Conrad K. B⸻

# MY FIRST CAR BOOK: DISCOVERING BRANDS AND LOGOS

**ALFA ROMEO**

**Alfa Romeo** is a prestigious Italian brand that produces sports cars. The company was founded by Alexandre Darracq in 1906 in Portello near Milan, where the company's headquarters is now located. Throughout its history, it has produced, inter alia, trolleybuses and off-road vehicles, however, it was the sports models that made the brand very famous. The models marked with the QV symbol (Quadrifoglio Verde - green four-leaf clover) especially ensure that the heart beats faster. Alfa Romeo was the first brand to use, among others, direct injection of common rail fuel (1997), variable valve timing (1980), a spark-ignition engine with two spark plugs per cylinder (1914), and a 6-speed gearbox in a series production model (1967).

**Aston Martin** is a British manufacturer of sports and luxury cars. The company was founded in 1914 by Lionel Martin and Robert Bamford in Gaydon. These cars are characterized by an elegant line, rich equipment, and attention to the smallest details.

The uniqueness is added by the fact that all British brand cars are assembled by hand. The reliability of workmanship is evidenced by the fact that approx. 75% of the cars sold are still fit for use. Most of us know these exclusive cars from movies about the adventures of British secret agent James Bond.

Not without reason, because various models of Aston Martin "appeared" in 10 parts!

**ASTON MARTIN**

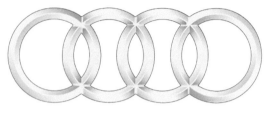

**Audi** begins its history at the beginning of the 20th century when in 1910 August Horch founded his company after numerous complications. The four rings are a symbol of the merger of 4 brands in 1932: Audi, Horch, Wanderer, and DKW.

The well-known motto of the brand "Advantage through technology" appeared for the first time in 1971. At every step, German engineers tried to convince us of the correctness of this saying. In March 1980 in Geneva, Audi presented the world's first passenger car with 4-wheel drive - the Quattro model.

In 1985, Audi was the second car manufacturer in the world, after Porsche, to produce fully galvanized bodies.

**AUDI**

**Bentley** is a UK-based luxury sports car manufacturer based in Cheshire, Crewe. Its founder in 1919 was Walter Owen Bentley, who dreamed of building a racing car that would be unbeatable in its class. He presented his first car, the Bentley 3 Liter, in 1921, but it took 3 years to see his success when he won the Le Mans race. In 1931, the brand was bought by Rolls-Royce. Post-war models, apart from a few cases, were just sports versions of the Rolls-Royce until the 1990s.

**BENTLEY**

**BMW**

**BMW** is one of the most popular car brands today. However, German engineers did not design cars from the very beginning. The plant was founded in 1913 by Gustav Otto and Karl Rapp and was first involved in the production of airplanes and motorcycles. At that time, the BMW company logo was created, which shows a stylized circle of the propeller in the colors of Bavaria. It was not until 1929 that BMW constructed its first mass-produced car - the BMW 3/15. The company owes its greatest development to Eberhard von Kuenheim. He made BMW important not only in Europe but all over the world. Thanks to the release of models such as the 3.0 CSL, M1, or M3 E30 by the BMW Motorsport department, our pulse has soared more than once.

**Bugatti** is a French manufacturer of exclusive sports and racing cars. The founder of the brand in 1909 was Ettore Bugatti. His cars won almost all major races before World War II. Unfortunately, when it broke out, Ettore was forced to stop production, and as a result of his death in 1947, he never returned to it. To reactivate the brand, in 1987 the Italian Romano Artioli founded the company Bugatti Automobili SpA in Campogalliano. There is a reason why the most recognizable model today is the Veyron. The Super Sport version holds the title of the fastest mass-produced car.

**BUGATTI**

**BUICK**

**Buick** is an American brand that produces luxury passenger cars. It was founded in 1903 by designer and inventor David Dunbar Buick in Detroit, where the company's headquarters is still located today and is one of the oldest still operating American automotive companies. One of the first owners of the brand was William C. Durant, among others. the creator of the now great General Motors concern, to which Buick belongs.

In GM's offer, it is positioned higher than Opel, but lower than the flagship Cadillac. The three shields in the brand's logo refer to the coat of arms of the noble family of the company's founder.

**Cadillac** is an American manufacturer of luxury passenger cars. The company was founded by Henry Leland in 1902 in Detroit. From the very beginning, the brand attached great importance to the quality of production, which was very profitable for them, because it is associated with the highest quality and luxury to this day. Their cars were driven by singers, actors, and, most of all, US presidents. American constructors showed off their innovativeness almost at every step, installing their models for the first time, among others. electric lighting, electric starter, V8 engine, air conditioning, and headlights switched on from the dashboard.

**CADILLAC**

**Chevrolet** is an American car brand belonging to General Motors concern. It was founded by the Swiss racing driver and mechanic Louis Chevrolet and William Durant. There are many versions of the company's logo, but the most likely one is when Durant was inspired by a wallpaper design in a French hotel where he stayed during a trip in 1908 and tore off a piece of it to show to friends, thinking it would be a good hallmark for a car brand.

## CHEVROLET

**Chrysler** is one of the most popular car brands in the USA. It was founded in 1925 by Walter Chrysler in Auburn Hills. Chrysler has had several successes in innovating the automotive market. In 1951, a prototype of the V8 Hemi engine was created, and for many years Chrysler was very successful - in 1987 it acquired American Motor Corporation, and in 1998 it merged with Daimler-Benz. In addition to passenger cars, the concern produced SUVs, sports cars, pick-ups, and vans.

**CHRYSLER**

**Citroen** is a French brand of passenger cars, vans, and trucks was founded by engineer Andre Citroën in 1919. Citroën models have always been distinguished by their original, cosmic appearance, unusual interior, and interesting technological solutions. Many of them won the Car of the Year title, incl. GS (1971), CX (1975) or XM (1990).

## CITROEN

**Dacia** is a Romanian producer of passenger cars and vans. The company was founded in 1966 (although its origins date back to 1943) in Pitesti, and its name comes from "Dacia", the name of the land inhabited by the ancestors of Romanians.

In 1999, cooperation with Renault was renewed, which bought the majority of the shares of the Romanian brand.

The breakthrough year for the company was 2004 when they launched the Logan model. It broke all records in terms of Dacia production volume. Since then, the Romanian brand has experienced a revival, and its numerous models find many customers around the world.

**DACIA**

**Dodge** is an American brand that produces passenger cars. Its beginning dates back to 1897 when brothers John and Horace Dodge founded their own company – Dodge Brothers Bicycle & Machine Factory, where bicycles and machine parts were manufactured. A very important event for the brand was the launch of cars with the V8 HEMI engine in the 1950s. Thanks to him, the brand achieved numerous successes in NASCAR class races. In 1966, they presented the Charger – today considered one of the icons of the brand. Thus, they began the era of the so-called "Muscle cars".

# DODGE

**Ferrari** is an Italian manufacturer of luxury sports cars. The headquarters are located in the city of Maranello. The company was founded in 1946 by the legendary Enzo Ferrari from Modena, who was a racing driver. There is a black steed in the Ferrari logo, which refers to the emblem of the plane of Francesco Baracca, a pilot from the First World War.

The manufacturer was very successful in motorsport, including the most prestigious series – Formula 1. Ferrari cars set trends in the super sports car segment. They compete on the market with brands such as Lamborghini, Porsche, Aston Martin, and Maserati.

**FERRARI**

**FIAT** is an Italian manufacturer of passenger cars and vans (and once also trucks, agricultural machinery, and airplanes).
The company was founded in 1899 by Giovanni Aneglli in Turin.
A year later, their first model, 3 1/2 HP, was released.
The brand developed rapidly and by 1939 it already had
5 factories. The brand is popular in Europe, especially very much
in Italy.

## FIAT

**Ford** is an American company that produces passenger cars, vans, and trucks. It was founded by one of the most important people in the history of motorization - Henry Ford in 1903 in Detroit. A month after its foundation, the first car is built - the A model, but it was the 1908 T model that was a real hit. Over 15 million copies were produced for 19 years, which is why in 1913, Ford was the first in the world to introduce mass production, thanks to which a new car rolled off the line every 10 seconds. In 1964, the Americans created one of the most recognizable cars in the world - the Mustang. From him began the term "Pony car", a car with a compact body, sporty design, and powerful engine.

**FORD**

**GMC** is an American company that produces sport utility vehicles, SUVs, and trucks. The origins of the brand date back to 1902, when the Rapid Motor Vehicle Company was founded by Maks Grabowski, one of the first truck manufacturers. During the war, their CCKW model (with a capacity of up to 2.5 tons!) was one of the basic trucks in the American army. For a long time, models had such markings on their bodies, until in 1996 it was finally decided to remove the word Truck from the name.

GMC

**Honda** is a Japanese brand that produces passenger cars, vans, motorcycles, and engines for various types of construction and agricultural machinery. It was established in 1948 on the initiative of Soichiro Honda in Tokyo. The brand's first vehicle was a bicycle powered by a 50cc engine. The next motorcycle was launched a year later. It did not start producing Honda cars until 1953 - the first was the T360. In 1971, the Honda Gold Wing was introduced - the first motorcycle with reverse gear. A year later, the Japanese decided to launch the first mass-produced compact car - the Civic. It achieved huge market success, and 9 generations of this car have been manufactured to this day.

**HONDA**

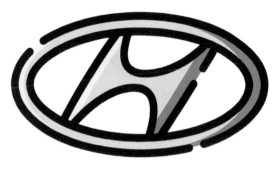

**HYUNDAI**

**Hyundai** is a South Korean automotive concern. Its origins date back to 1947 when Chung Ju-Yung founded Hyundai Engineering and Construction (then the largest construction company). It was not until 20 years later that the Hyundai Motor Company was founded to produce cars. The name means modernity in the native language (Hyeondae), and the logo symbolizes a handshake of two people. The first car was built a year later. It was called Cotina and was based on the Ford model - Cortina. The Pony was their first self-constructed vehicle (1974), but the collaboration with Ford continued until 1985. The company is constantly developing and modernizing its range of vehicles, focusing mainly on their failure-free operation.
In many cases, it surpasses its rivals from Europe or the United States in this respect.

**Infiniti** is a Japanese brand of luxury cars owned by Nissan. Its story begins in 1985 when the idea to create a luxury brand from scratch was born. The name was chosen 2 years later, it means "infinity". In fact, the creation of the brand was Nissan's response to the Acura (luxury Honda). The first Infiniti car entered the market in 1989, the same as the first Lexus model – an exclusive version of Toyota. Initially, the Japanese sold their cars only on the North American market.

**INFINITI**

**Jaguar** - British brand of luxury passenger cars, founded in 1922 by Sir William Lyons, but originally called the Swallow Sidecar Company and sold motorcycle sidecars. Lyons' first car, the two-door SS1 limousine, entered the market in 1932.

In the 1950s, the brand began to compete in car races, including the 24 Hours of Le Mans. A year after the typical sports car, the XK120C, was presented, Jaguar took its first victory at Le Mans, and the collaboration with Dunlop resulted in the creation of disc brakes, which turned out to be the perfect recipe for further wins. In addition, the brand triumphed in France 5 more times.

## JAGUAR

**Jeep** is an American brand of off-road cars, produced by the Willys company since 1941. In the beginning, they produced their vehicles for the army, and after the war, they started selling civilian cars. The prototype - Willys Quad was built in just ...
49 days! To this day, it is one of the most popular vehicles of World War II. In 1950, the Willys company reserved the name of the Jeep, but the first civilian model appeared in 1945 - the CJ2A. In 1962, the American manufacturer introduced the first automatic transmission in a 4x4 vehicle It was also the first 4x4 model with independent front-wheel suspension, but the most popular was the Wrangler and Grand Cherokee.

# Jeep

**JEEP**

**KIA** is a Korea's oldest automotive company produces passenger cars and vans. It started its activity in 1944, but then it operated under the name of Kyungsung Precision Industries and was involved in the production of bicycle parts. Before the release of their first commercial vehicle in 1962, the K-360, Koreans also produced motorcycles. Since the 1970s, many Kii models were built under a license from Mazda. In 1997, the company was on the verge of bankruptcy. It was then that Hyundai came to the rescue, buying Kia shares two years later and creating the Hyundai company - the Kia Automotive Group. Currently, the brand is dynamically developing and becomes a potential competitor for renowned Western European brands.

**KIA**

**Lamborghini** - an Italian brand that produces luxury sports cars, as well as agricultural tractors. The company was founded in 1948 by Ferruccio Lamborghini, who initially made a fortune in tractor production.

It is known for a long time that the biggest rival of Lamborghini is another Italian brand - Ferrari. The idea to create a supercar was born after Ferrucci's quarrel with Enzo Ferrari. Lamborghini, as a wealthy person, drove a car with a black steed on the hood. However, he was not entirely happy with him, and when he suggested some changes to Enzo, he laughed at him. Thus, in 1963 a Lamborghini 350 GTV with a V12 engine was created, which outperformed the cars from Modena.

3 years later, Miura was founded, which made the brand famous all over the world. She was vicious and difficult to drive but captivated with her elegance and subtle lines.

**LAMBORGHINI**

**LANCIA**

**Lancia** - an Italian brand of passenger cars, founded in 1906 in Turin by Vincenzo Lancia and Claudio Fogolina. The Lambda model, created in 1922, was Lancia's first major market success. Among the innovative solutions that appeared, others self-supporting bodies and independent front-wheel suspension. The Astura (1931) had an engine suspension that reduced the transmission of vibrations to the car, and the 1933 Augusta was the first sedan with hydraulic brakes. Lancia models were known from the beginning for their elegance and sensual lines. Automotive fans will especially remember models such as the Stratos, 037, or Delta, to which the brand owes numerous successes in motorsport and is still the most successful team in the history of WRC.

**Land Rover** is a British brand of off-road vehicles founded in 1948. Initially, their models were produced by Rover, but in 1975 Land Rover became an independent brand. The first model was Series I, which was exported to 70 countries. It was to be used in agriculture and light industry, but the military also used it. 10 years later, the second generation of this model appeared, and by 1985 a third one was made. His successor was the world-famous Defender. The first Range Rover is born in 1970. It was better equipped and had a 3.5-liter V8 engine that allowed it to accelerate to 160 kmh (100 mph). The most recognizable models today, apart from Defender, are Discovery (premiered in 1988) and Freelander (1997).

**LAND ROVER**

**LEXUS**

**Lexus** - Japanese brand of luxury passenger cars owned by Toyota. In 1983, the president of the concern from the Land of the Rising Sun announced a plan to create an exclusive line of cars that could compete with limousines from Western Europe. The brand name was to be associated with luxury and elegance. Lexus' first sports car, the SC model with a 4-liter V8 engine, was launched two years later, and the LX sport utility vehicle, based on the Toyota Land Cruiser, in 1996. In 2006, the company was the first to install an automatic parking system in its flagship LS model. The Japanese charmed the international jury with the show, where the same model parked between the pillars set from champagne glasses without the driver's help and they decided to award it the World Car Of The Year 2007 title.

**Lincoln** is an American brand that produces luxury passenger cars. It was founded in 1917 by Henry Leland in tribute to President Abraham Lincoln. In 1922, Lincoln was acquired by Ford, being to this day the most luxurious brand in the Ford concern and the biggest competitor of Cadillac from GM.

In 1939, the legendary Continental model was created, which had as many as 9 generations! It was also where US President John F. Kennedy was shot in 1963. Continental replaced the Town Car model in 2002. The brand's first SUV, one of the most recognizable Lincoln models today, the Navigator model, was presented in 1998, and its third generation is being produced since 2007.

**LINCOLN**

**Lotus** is a British automotive company that produces sports and racing cars. It was founded in 1952 by Colin Chapman, one of the most acclaimed sports car designers in history.

The brand became popular thanks to participation in Formula 1 races. Lotus competed in them continuously for 60 years, from 1954, winning the world championship seven times. British cars are characterized by simple workmanship, great handling, and low weight. The most famous models of the brand are Esprit (1976-2004; known, among others, from the James Bond movie), Elise - produced since 1995, Exige - a stronger version of Elise, and Evora, which entered the market in 2008.

## LOTUS

**Maserati** - an Italian company that produces sports and racing cars. The origins of the brand date back to 1914, when one of the six brothers of the Maserati family, Alfieri, established his workshop in Bologna, Officine Alfieri Maserati. Soon the rest of the brothers joined him, except for one – Mario, who became an artist and is credited with designing the brand's logo. He drew inspiration from the Neptune Fountain in his hometown. In 1958, the first road Maserati model was produced – the 3500 GT, and the first four-door model – the Quattroporte in 1963. The most popular models of the brand are, among others Quattroporte with six generations, and GranTurismo.

**MASERATI**

**MAZDA**

**Mazda** is a Japanese brand that mainly produces passenger cars. The company derives from the small company Toyo Kogyo Co. founded in 1920 by Jyujiro Matsuda. In the 1960s, Mazda began experimenting with a Wankel engine in which a piston spun inside a cylinder. Thus, in 1967, their first model with the same bike was created - the 110S Cosmo. In 1978, the RX-7 model debuted, which was a great success and reached the 3rd generation. The last one is especially favored by tuners from Japan and the USA. Its engine with a capacity of only 1.3 liters and with the help of 2 turbochargers generated up to 280 HP in series! Mazda saw one of its greatest successes when it introduced the MX-5 to the world in 1989, a small two-seater roadster. Thanks to its low weight, good balance, and relatively low power, it gave great satisfaction from driving.

**McLaren** Automotive (formerly McLaren Cars) is a division of the British company McLaren Group, dealing with the production of sports cars based on Formula 1 technology. It was founded in 1989 by Ron Dennis in Woking, but the Formula 1 racing team was formed in 1963. The first civilian McLaren car was the F1 model, which was presented in 1991. It was equipped with a V12 engine with a power of 627 HP, it did not have a power steering system, braking assistance, or traction control. All of this is done to get as light as possible. It took about 3 seconds to reach 100 kmh (60 mph) and by 2005 it held the title of the fastest series-produced car - it accelerated to 386 kmh (239 mph). The brand competes with Ferrari, Porsche, and Lamborghini.

**MCLAREN**

**MERCEDES-BENZ**

**Mercedes-Benz** is a German brand of cars produced by Daimler AG concern. Passenger cars, vans, trucks, and buses are produced under the three-pointed star badge. Its beginning dates back to 1883, when Karl Benz, Max Rose, and Fredrich W. Esslinger founded Benz & Co. The name Mercedes comes from the name of Mercedes Jellinek, daughter of Emil Jellink, representative of Daimler. The paths of Benz and Daimler's companies converged as a result of changes in the German economy and the Daimler-Benz company was officially established in 1926. Mercedes is distinguished above all by quality, innovation, and safety, which is why it is considered one of the most prestigious brands in the world. The brand has also achieved numerous successes in many racing classes, incl. including Formula 1.

**Mitsubishi** is a Japanese company founded in 1870 by Yataro Iwasaki. in the aviation industry, defense industry, and what interests us most - automotive. The name means "3 diamonds" in Japanese and it reflects this in its logo. Automotive fans are particularly fond of the sporty version of the Lancer, Evolution, which has been competing with another legend, the Subaru Impreza, in the World Rally Championship for years. The popular "EVO", however, appeared on the market only in 1992, saw its 10th generation, and its end in 2015.

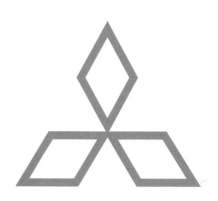

**MITSUBISHI**

**NISSAN**

**Nissan** is a Japanese manufacturer of passenger cars, trucks, and buses belonging to the Nissan Motor Co. The origins of the brand date back to 1911, when Masujiro Hashimoto founded the Kwaishinsha company in Tokyo. It wasn't until 1934 that the company changed its name to Nissan. After the war, the company was engulfed in a crisis, from which the concern emerged in cooperation with British Austin. Soon after, Nissan became the second-largest car manufacturer in Japan. In 1989, Nissan launched its luxury brand for the US market - Infiniti. Since 1999, the Japanese have been cooperating with French Renault. The most popular Nissan models are the Micra, Qashqai, Skyline (especially loved by tuners and drifters), and its successor - the GT-R.

**Opel** is one of the most popular German automotive brands. The company was founded by Adam Opel in 1862 in Rüsselheim. Initially, it was involved in the production of sewing machines, and later also bicycles. After the founder died in 1895, the company was taken over by his wife and five sons. After 4 years, the first Opel-Patent-MotorWagen was produced on a chassis by Friedrich Lutzman. The first Opel model of its design was made in 1902 - the 10 / 12PS model. In 1989, Opel was the first manufacturer in Europe to introduce a catalytic converter as standard equipment. The most popular models of the German brand were, among others Kadett, Corsa, Vectra, and Omega. In Great Britain, Opel models are sold under the name Vauxhall, and in Australia - Holden.

**OPEL**

**PEUGEUOT**

**Peugeot** is a French company that manufactures cars, scooters, and bicycles, and in the past also trucks and motorcycles. It was established in Sochaux and was founded by Jean Pierre Peugeot. The first car, the Serpollet-Peugeot, with a steam engine appeared in 1889, but it was only the Daimler internal combustion engine vehicle presented in 1891 that proved to be the right move. In 1929, the 201 model began a series of three-digit markings with a zero in the middle. The first number indicates the class and the last number is the next series. In 1948, the first post-war Peugeot 203 model was released, which was produced until 1960. In 1959, a radiator fan was used for the first time, preparing cars for the coming traffic jams.

**Porsche** is a German sports car manufacturer based in Stuttgart. The founder of the company was in 1931 Ferdinand Porsche, an engineer who had previously gained experience with Daimler. The first vehicle named after him was created as early as 1938, but the first mass-produced car with the Porsche logo was made in 1948 - the 356 model. The most popular Porsche model - the 911, was made in 1963. The car turned out to be a world hit, achieving success not only in sales but also in sports. The 911 was the first car to win the famous Paris-Dakar Rally without being an off-road car. Currently, it is one of the brand's most recognizable cars. The success of the 911 was attempted to be replicated with models such as the 924/944, 928, and 968, but none of them succeeded.

**PORSCHE**

**RENAULT**

**Renault** is a French automotive brand that produces cars and trucks. The company was founded in 1899 by brothers Louis, Fernand, and Marcel Renault. Soon more models were created, already with units designed by the company's owners. The first post-war model was the 4CV, and in 1961 it was replaced by the longest-produced (as many as 28 years) the 4 model.

The Renault 16, on the other hand, was the forerunner of today's family models. It was the first Renault car to win the Car of the Year title in 1966. It was also the first car in the world with a hatchback body. The Car of the Year titles was also won by the Clio (1991 and 2006) and Scenic (1996) models. Seat belts have been fitted as standard on all models since 1970.

**Rolls-Royce** is an English manufacturer of luxury limousines. The idea of a collaboration between Charles Rolls and Henry Royce arose in 1904 over lunch. From the very beginning, the brand was also involved in the production of aircraft engines, which contributed to the division of the brand into two branches in 1973. In 1906, the Silver Ghost model was designed. It was equipped with a 7-liter six-cylinder bottom valve engine with a power of less than 50 HP. A characteristic feature of the English brand is a statuette on the hood - Spirit of Ecstasy, which is synonymous with wealth and the highest quality. In the latest models, for safety reasons, it is hidden by a special button under the flap. Today, Rolls-Royce is considered one of the most exclusive and luxurious brands in the world.

**SEAT**

**SEAT** is a Spanish brand of passenger cars. It was founded in 1950 by the National Institute of Industry, a banking organization, and the Fiat concern. It was the Italian cars that served as a model for the first Seat models. The first model was 1400, and its production started in 1953 in Barcelona. In 1980, Fiat sold its shares to the National Institute of Industry, making Seat Spain's first independent car manufacturer. At that time, the model range was heavily modernized, and models such as Ibiza, Marbella, and Malaga appeared. In 1986, Volkswagen bought 51% of Seat's shares. In the 1990s, they rose to 99%, when the first models appeared, in which German technology was hidden under the body designed by Giugiaro.

**Skoda** is a Czech company producing passenger cars. The origins of the brand date back to 1895, when the mechanic Vaclav Laurin and the accountant Vaclav Klement founded the Laurin & Klement company producing bicycles, and from 1898 also motorcycles. They built their first prototype car in 1901, and serial production lasted for 27 years. In 1964, Škoda launched a family car - the 1000 MB model. Its engine was located at the rear - the experience of such cars as Fiat 600 or Porsche 356 was used here. Cooperation with Volkswagen began in 1991, when Škoda joined the group of the German brand. The first model of the Czech brand to use German technology was Felicia in 1994.

**SKODA**

**Subaru** is a Japanese brand of passenger cars and delivery vans. The history of the company begins in 1953 when after the war 6 concerns were united into one called Fuji Heavy Industries, symbolized by 6 stars in the company's logo. In 1954, the first prototype was called P-1, and a year later the model was called 1500. In 1992, the famous Impreza was presented. Colin McRae, behind the wheel, has repeatedly won the world title in rallies, and thus the Subaru Impreza has become an inseparable element of rallies. Thanks to them, the model gained popularity all over the world.

## SUBARU

**Suzuki** is a Japanese brand of passenger cars, trucks, motorcycles, and engines. The company was founded in 1909 when Michio Suzuki founded a weaving equipment factory in the seaside town of Hamamatsu. After almost 30 years, Michio realized that his company had to develop in other areas as well, so in 1937 he started designing the car and after 2 years he had a few prototypes. 1970 is an important year for the brand.

Then, the first generation of the Jimmy off-road model, which was a global success, had its premiere. In 1983, the sale of the one-liter Swift passenger car, which was very successful on the market, starts. The SX4 and Vitara are also popular models.

**SUZUKI**

**TESLA**

**Tesla** is an American brand of luxury and sports electric cars. The name of the company comes from the name of Nikola Tesla, a Serbian engineer, and inventor of many electrical appliances. The company was founded in 2003 by Elon Musk. Work on the first model, the Roadster, lasted for 5 years. In 2008 it was put into production. Its performance rivaled many petrol-powered sports vehicles. A year later, a vehicle with a liftback body was presented. On one charge, it was to be able to cover a distance of 300 miles and at the same time have sporty performance. Its production started in 2012 and the vehicle was called Model S. The company is gaining more and more popularity due to the electrification of the automotive industry.

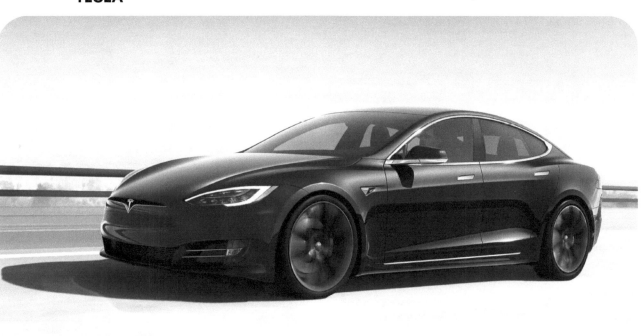

**Toyota** is a Japanese automotive brand, founded by Sakichi Toyoda in 1918, and his company initially operated in the clothing industry. The automotive department was established in 1933 and the first prototype was established two years later. Production of the first model – AA, started in 1936. In 1966, the first generation of one of the most popular models of the brand – Corolla was created. In 2013, the 11th generation of this model was presented. In 1992, the fourth generation of the sports Supra module was created, which was especially liked by tuners. In 2014, Toyota launched the Mirai, the first production hydrogen fuel cell car in Japan. In 2015, it also appeared in some European countries. Toyota is one of the largest automotive concerns in the world. In addition, it also owns the Lexus and Daihatsu brands.

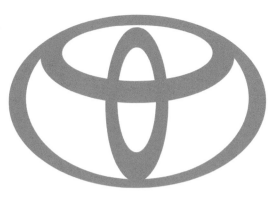

**TOYOTA**

**VOLKSWAGEN**

**Volkswagen** is a German brand of passenger cars and vans belongs to the Volkswagenwerk Aktien-Gesellschaft (VAG) concern. Its story begins in 1931 when the Zündapp company asked Ferdinand Porsche to create a cheap car. In 1934, on the orders of Adolf Hitler, Ferdinand presented the first design of the legendary Beetle. It was supposed to be a cheap family car, and Hitler baptized it as "the people's car." By 2003, when its production was officially discontinued, a total of over 21.5 million copies had been made.

In 1973, another very popular model was presented - the Passat. Right after him, Golf made its debut. It was supposed to repeat the Beetle's success, and it did. The Volkswagen concern includes brands such as Audi, Skoda, Seat, Porsche, Lamborghini, Bugatti, and Bentley.

**Volvo** is a Swedish brand of passenger cars, trucks, construction machinery, and engines. The company name means "to turn around" in Swedish. Their first car was the ÖV4, the production of which began in 1927. The founders wanted their vehicles to be of high quality and technically advanced. In 1966, the 144 models was created, which was considered the most technologically advanced car in the world. The car had controlled crumple zones, disc brakes on all wheels, and seat belts also appeared on the rear seat.

In 1999, half of the rights to Volvo were taken over by Ford, and after 11 years the new owner of Volvo Car Corporation was Chinese Geely. Currently produced models have a letter in front of the number which denotes the type of the vehicle's bodywork: C - convertible or coupé; S - sedan; V - station wagon; XC - off-road model.

**VOLVO**

# Check also:

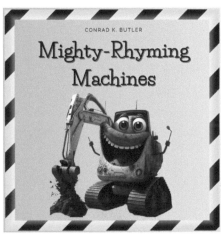

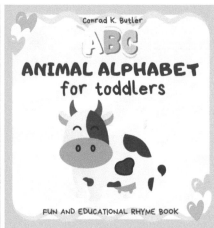

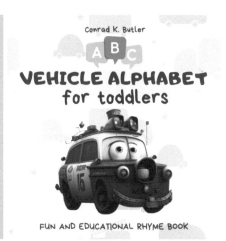

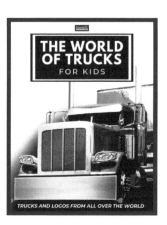

# and much more!